Alexia Parks

Leadership Based On The Female Brain

10 Traits

Leaders

Of

Power

And Great

Courage

10 Truths About the Female Brain That
Will Forever Change Your World

AlexiaParks.com

ALEXIA PARKS

PRAISE FOR 10 TRAITS

””

"*I consider Alexia Parks a brilliant thought leader.*"
- **Remy Arteaga**, Executive Director, Stanford Latino Entrepreneurship Initiative

””

"Terrific! Very Powerful."
- **Bud Sorenson**, former President of Babson College, and Acting Dean of the CU-Boulder School of Business

””

"*To date, our project received the best reviews for impact and sustainability in the whole of Africa, thanks to Alexia's diligent mentorship.*"
- **Rehmah Kasule,** Goldman Sachs/Fortune Global Women Leaders Award Winner 2014; Founder - CEDA-Uganda.org

””

"*Provocative! 5-STARS*" *"In today's world..., women are superior in social bonding, fostering diversity, expressing emotions and having empathy for the plights of others."*
- **Laurence Kirshbaum**, former Vice-President and head of the NY Publishing Office of Amazon.com

””

"*Wow! THAT WAS ONE OF THE BEST TALKS* that I have ever attended (I have been to 100's if not 1000's). Not only was the content excellent, but you are a superb presenter. I loved the way that you interacted with and involved the audience."
- **Malcolm Fraser M.D.**

10 TRAITS - LEADERS OF POWER AND COURAGE

"*Alexia Parks is* **leading** *new thinking in the area of social change and the role of women in our modern world.*"

-**Margaret Manning**, Founder of Boomerly, and the SixtyandMe online.

" "

"*Alexia is a visionary pioneer.*"

- **Rajeev Rawat, Co-Founder and CEO BI Results LLC**

" "

"*This weekend I had the opportunity to attend the 10 TRAITS Science-Based Leadership Training by Alexia Parks. It was a wonderful training and one of the pieces is the keynote by Alexia on 'Darwin's Remarkable Women.' It's a fascinating talk on the particular traits of the female brain and how those traits have evolved over time and are now essential leadership skills for moving work forward in today's world.*"

- **Andréa Giron,** *Manager of Audience Insights, Denver Museum of Nature & Science*

" "

"*I so appreciate the work you do and pray that it pays off for all of us sooner rather than later.*"

- **Claudine Schneider**, former Congresswoman from Rhode Island, Co-Founded the Competitiveness Caucus in the U.S. Congress. Gave a briefing to Margaret Thatcher. Co-hosted the CNN coverage of the Senate Chief Justice Confirmation hearings on Clarence Thomas. Participated with Prince Charles in a BBC film on Climate Change.

" "

"*The response from participants has been overwhelmingly positive. I'm told that some women were even in tears at the end; some asked 'When is the next event?'*"

- **Anne Zonne Parker**, Professor, Environmental Studies, Naropa University.

ALEXIA PARKS

"I am on the steering committee for our Women in Leadership group at a leading Life Science and High Technology company and I appreciate your work."
Lori Cordova-Oistad

"

"Alexia presents an interesting argument for female leadership, referencing biological evolution, cultural anthropology, and more."
- **Sheryl Winarick**, Immigration Attorney whose clients include TED (and TEDsters across the globe), Oxfam... individuals and "families who risk leaving everything familiar behind with Hope and Faith in a bright future."

"

"Thank you Alexia for holding the space for all of us to come into our power in a much higher way together."
- **Maestra Antonia Joy Wilson**, Artistic Director, CEO & Conductor of Global Arts Center: Multimedia Symphony.

"

"I am excited for your work and look forward to supporting it as we all move forward." - **Seleyn DeYarus, Executive Director at FearLess Revolution**

"

"Thanks Alexia — These are the conversations we need to be having! Please don't hesitate to ask if there is anything [we] can do to support your efforts!"
- **Michelle Meyer**, Founder, GirlAuthentic

"

"Sometimes you meet a individual that sparkles. Alexia is just one such person, shining her light and wisdom wherever she goes! Her wisdom and brilliance is contagious. Encountering Alexia, and having the great honor of spending time with her, is a life-changing event."

- **Therese Hartmann**, President, World Family Foundation, Vice President, Ojai Education Foundation (OEF).

10 TRAITS - LEADERS OF POWER AND COURAGE

"My mother/ Alexia has always been the most positive, courageous woman I've known. She has always been a visionary. She has shown me how to be fearless in pursuing whatever goals I set for myself by leading the way herself with persistence, positivity, and bravery. You're lucky if you know her and even more lucky if you have the opportunity to be close enough to be touched by her warmth and luminosity."

- Hillary Griffith @hillarygriffith

99

"**When I was five** my tree house was forty feet off the ground. My mother often sat reading at the bottom while I bear hugged my way up into my hanging hide out.

When I was nineteen my mother came to watch me climb. I free soloed a lot back then and was comfortable several hundred feet off the ground on a vertical face with out a rope. Again my mother seemed comfortable siting amid the jagged talus boulders below, watching.

I few years later I was a professional climber and by many accounts one of the best in the sport and a "founder" of modern technique.

Reflecting back on this and the role my mother played in my achievements I can say that for myself and many others I believe the domain our dreams inhabit is a fragile one.

Often our drive is lost and our goals relinquished prematurely because of the criticism or skepticism of a parent or mentor. In this respect I have been very lucky to have had the mother I have. Never doubting, always supportive and confident in my abilities even when a slip or lapse of concentration would have meant my demise.

Her unflinching, positive optimism reinforced not only my belief in my own talent but also in the endeavor I have dedicated my life to, the sport of rock climbing now main stream but in my youth one very much on the fringe. - Christian Griffith, First born. VERVEClimbing.com

ALEXIA PARKS

Alexia Parks 10 TRAITS – <u>Leadership Training Programs</u>
<u>Based On The Female Brain</u> (CLICK HERE)
<u>AlexiaParks.com</u>

BOOKS by Alexia Parks

<u>10 TRAITS of Leaders of Power and Courage</u>

<u>10 Traits of Women of Power and Courage</u> (1st, 2nd, 3rd editions)

<u>Parkinomics: 8 GREAT Ways to Thrive in the New Economy</u> (Amazon Bestseller)

<u>Dr Joel's Be Super Fit™ for Life!</u>

<u>Focus on Success: A 10 Step Mentoring System for Schools</u>

<u>An American GULAG: Secret P.O.W. Camps for Teens</u>

<u>10 Golden Rules That Guide Loving Families (English/Spanish)</u>

<u>Rapid Evolution: Seven Words That Will Change Your Life Forever!</u>

10 Golden Rules That Guide Teacher-Mentors (2015)

How Changing Your Name Can Change Your Life (2016)

<u>How Love Heals</u> (Cancer) (<u>Colorectal Cancer</u>)

<u>People Heaters: How to Keep Warm in Winter</u>

WEB: <u>ALEXIAPARKS.COM</u> twitter: @alexiaparks

No part of this book may be used or reproduced in any manner whatsoever without writ-ten permission, except by a reviewer who may quote brief passages in a review.

TheEducationExchange.org – (SAN #253-0872) – Publisher
1st Edition: © 2012; 2nd Edition © 2014; 3rd Edition © 2015; 4th Edition © 2016

Based in Boulder, CO, and Ojai, California USA - 303-443-3697

10 TRAITS - LEADERS OF POWER AND COURAGE

"It's not what you call me, but what I answer to."

African Woman's Proverb

"My successor may be a woman. If the circumstances are such that *a female Dalai Lama* is more useful, then *a female Dalai Lama* will come"

The Dalai Lama

"The fastest way to change society is to mobilize the women of the world."

Charles Malik, former President of the United Nations General Assembly

"If ever the world sees a time when women shall come together purely and simply for the benefit of humankind, it will be a power such as the world has never known."

Matthew Arnold, 19th Century philosopher

ALEXIA PARKS

ABOUT THE AUTHOR

Alexia Parks is recognized by those who know of her work as a though leader and world expert on a new model of leadership and empowerment based on 10 powerful leadership traits found in the female brain. She calls her ground-breaking discovery: the New Science of the Female Brain.

The New Science of the Female Brain draws upon 40-years worth of research across a dozen fields of science including neurobiology, split brain research and both physical and cultural anthropology.

As a science journalist, an award-winning entrepreneur, virtual mentor with the United Nations, and founder of the **10 TRAITS Institute**, Alexia Parks has developed training programs based on neuroplasticity, neurogenesis, and epigenetics, to help the next generation of leaders activate their full potential.

She is also a Huffington Post blogger, and Newsweek's "One of 50 people who matter most on the Internet (1995)" for her launch of the first electronic democracy voting system on the Internet. See: Wikipedia.

In 2000, Parks pioneered **an educational innovation**: a national mentor-teacher training program for schools called **Focus on Success**. She was also the first accredited blogger for the United Nations Framework Convention on Climate Change, Bali 2007. An international speaker and author, Alexia Parks formerly wrote for the national desk of The Washington Post, was a NYC magazine publisher, and served as communications director for an organization that represented 100 Sunday Metropolitan newspapers.

In 2014, Parks founded the 10 TRAITS Leadership Institute to engage and mobilize a new generation of leaders. It is the first and only leadership training program in the world based on this new field of science and aligned with how the FEMALE brain actually works. The historic launch of the **Alexia Parks 10 TRAITS Institute** was sponsored by Naropa University, and cross promoted by the Deming Center, University of Colorado – Boulder. Colorado State University offered continuing education credit. WEB: AlexiaParks.com

Table of Contents

Introduction...11

A Paradigm Shift 13

Who We Really Are.... 19

The Greatest Revolution in Human History.......................23

Chart: 10 Major Changes in Human Lifestyle.....................27
10 Major Leadership Traits...36
The Chart of Opposites...39
Trait #1 The Collaborative Leader.......................................41

Trait #2 The Nurturing Leader..47

Trait #3 The Expressive Leader...53

Trait #4 The Empathetic Leader..57

Trait #5 The Healing Power of Touch...................................59

Trait #6 The Compassionate Leader.....................................63

Trait #7 The Mindful Leader...67

Trait #8 The Environmental Leader.....................................71

Trait #9 The Prioritizing Leader..75

Trait #10 The Diplomatic Leader...77

What the World Needs Now...80
Rate Yourself: The 10 Traits of Leaders...............................83
Epilogue: Just Do THIS..85
Rwanda: A Case History...91
Resources...93

ALEXIA PARKS

10 TRAITS - LEADERS OF POWER AND COURAGE

INTRODUCTION

WELCOME to the first day of the rest of your life as a leader! I'm excited to share a ground-breaking discovery with you based on the New Science of the Female Brain. You possess 10 unique traits, and these 10 TRAITS just so happen to be the very traits that are needed in the world today, in order to manage the complexities of our volatile, interconnected world.

10 TRAITS offers the FIRST and ONLY model of leadership based on the mindful, compassionate, diplomatic Female Brain. Discover your unique talent as a leader and how to use it to become a socially conscious change agent. Upgrade your life to leadership!

This is a book for women, and for men who are interested in or curious about, 10 great traits found in both the male brain, and in the female brain.

As you will soon discover, t*he 10 major traits, found in the female brain are exactly the opposite of those found in the male brain. They are complementary, synergistic, and opposite.* And, these 10 traits just so happen to be the very traits that our leaders need today in order to successfully manage our complex, volatile world.

The truth is, these 10 important traits found in the female brain are needed in leadership roles at all levels of society, in dynamic partnership with men.

They represent *a major paradigm shift* that once understood, will forever change the way we look at women, politics, the workplace, and leadership.

In fact, these differences relate to every single human being on the planet, and every single human endeavor. They show up in the way we respond to relationships, the workplace, to politics, to economics, to the environment, to raising children, to adolescents, to marriage, and about 100 other major topics.

So, if there truly is a need to "Transform *the World*," there needs to be a quantum shift toward women in leadership roles at all levels of society.

As a woman, you are already endowed by Mother Nature with 10 natural leadership traits, and these 10 unique traits just so happen to be exactly what is needed to manage the complexities of today's volatile, interconnected world.

My job is simply to tell you how much power you have. You just don't know it!

So when you learn about the 10 traits, when you study them and meditate on them, when you focus your attention on these powerful traits that you already have, you will feel a new strength and confidence. You will regain the power that has always been yours.

10 TRAITS - LEADERS OF POWER AND COURAGE

A PARADIGM SHIFT

Every Monday morning - for 18 months - I attended a meeting in Kampala, Uganda. I met with a young woman named Rehmah Kasule, via SKYPE.

Rehmah's goal was to lift 200 young women out of the slums of Kampala, by teaching them micro-entrepreneurship, providing mentorship, and doing leadership training. And she was successful.

In 2014, she was flown from Africa to America where she won the Global Women Leaders 1st Place Award for her SLUM women project. She was also awarded $25,000 and had a chance to speak personally with Melinda Gates.

As a virtual mentor with the United Nations, assigned to work with Rehmah, my job had been to provide her with links to resources, creative ideas and solutions to problems as they arose, and ONE thing more. I reminded that each of the women she worked with has natural leadership traits.

And, these 10 special leadership traits found in the female brain just so happen to be exactly what's needed - urgently needed - in leadership today **to manage the complexities of our volatile, interconnected world**.

So, if you remember only one thing from reading *10 TRAITS of Leaders of*

ALEXIA PARKS

Power and Courage, remember this:

That when you learn about these 10 traits - which you already have, when you study them and focus on them, they will manifest as inner power, courage, and a will to lead.

The recognition of these natural leadership traits is based on 40 years of research across a dozen fields of science. These fields include neurobiology, the neuroplastic brain, split brain research, the psychology of perception, and both cultural and physical anthropology.

*When we come to understand this "New Science of the Female Brain" it forever changes the way we look at, and think about women.

 A brief history: So at the start of our journey into the hardwired brain, let me take a step back and tell you a little about myself, and how I came to make this ground-breaking discovery.

Throughout my whole life I have always been concerned with innovative ideas, accelerated learning techniques, and social impact technology that can help us, together, create a better world. It has been a lifetime journey, a lifetime quest.

10 TRAITS - LEADERS OF POWER AND COURAGE

My focus of interest has always included a combination of the environment, entrepreneurship, innovative technology, and communications. I've written about these issues in many different books and blogs, as well as created businesses that showcased real-world solutions.

However, the epiphany that I had as I began work on this book, is that it requires a constellation of many fields of human endeavor to address and resolve the many problems of the world, and especially those inequities that women face.

So this book represents a grand synthesis of documented and pieced together facts that form the basis of a **major paradigm shift** for humanity: a *new school of social thought called:* The New Science of the FEMALE Brain.

I am making this prediction, based on a quantum leap in my own thinking. It is a groundbreaking discovery made possible by piecing together significant findings from many different fields of research and science, and then applying them to men, women, and society at large.

ALEXIA PARKS

This discovery comes from the convergence of many fields including: a knowledge of cultural and physical anthropology, a knowledge of brain function in both men and women, the understanding of the physiology of hormones in both men and women, the psychology of perception in both men and women, and a broad knowledge of cultural studies, world history, and human endeavor.

And, the conclusion is this: That one of the most astonishing discoveries in human history that has been grossly overlooked, until now, is the fact that at this watershed moment in human history, the 10 life-affirming traits that are found in the FEMALE brain are exactly what is needed, **urgently needed**, to manage the complexities of our interconnected world.

While this may sound kind of dramatic, you will see by a review of the 10 different traits of men and women, in the chart found in Part II, that this is true. In fact, what the chart will show is that the traits found in the female brain are virtually the opposite of those found in the male brain. They are diametrically opposed, and have been so over millions of years.

10 TRAITS - LEADERS OF POWER AND COURAGE

It isn't that men are better than women, or women are better than men, it's simply that these traits are complementary, synergistic, and opposite.

Women think differently. This different way of looking at the world evolved in the female brain through evolutionary psychology.

This is one reason why adding more women to the decision-making process *makes* a difference: whether the decision is about taking more risks, solving some of the world's biggest environmental challenges, or facing issues of war, diplomacy, and peace.

More women in government, The Economist magazine reports, would shift government monies from a focus on weapons, tanks, and warfare, to healthcare, education, and the eradication of poverty.

How many women? Enough to make a difference!

ALEXIA PARKS

NOTES

10 TRAITS - LEADERS OF POWER AND COURAGE

WHO WE REALLY ARE

For 99.9% of human history we lived outdoors. The sky was our roof and the earth was our floor, and conditions were harsh. When it rained, we got wet. When it snowed, we got cold. Survival was constantly on our mind. And, there was never enough food. One could say that the mantra of the day was food-food-food. Food was everything. Food meant survival. Food was life itself.

At that time, our profession, both men and women, was that of the hunter-gatherer. And just like the name implies, it was the hunter and gatherer of food.

So men would go off on long hunts. They would rely on their dense muscles, their strong bones, their risk-taking, strength, and endurance to give them the advantage they needed to make a kill. Because of this, the male brain developed traits for **teamwork, competition, and the ability to focus on a single goal** without distraction.

ALEXIA PARKS

By contrast, as soon as women reached puberty, they were either pregnant or nursing and had children at their feet. It was the job of women to ensure the survival of the children, to gather nuts and seeds and firewood, and to know which trees bore edible fruit, and when it would ripen.

Women become a repository of critical life-affirming knowledge. They were also the economic equal of men.

However, due to the hardships our ancestors faced, and key to our story, is the fact that the average lifespan for both men and women was **only 25 years**. The stark reality of a 25-year-lifespan resulted in a clear-cut division of labor between men and women.

The Old Stone Age job of men required special skills. The men needed to work as a team, stay on the same wavelength, and focus on the same goal. They need to follow the prey, kill it, and then carry it home.

For many men, this "hands on" capture of food was no easy task. A study of human bones of Stone Age men reveals that some men may have suffered as many broken bones as a modern day rodeo rider.

Women also faced many risks. For women, the risks of childbirth were compounded by their nomadic lifestyle.

10 TRAITS - LEADERS OF POWER AND COURAGE

So the dichotomy that developed between men and women - that is, the differences between men and women - can be explained by 10 special traits found in both the male and female brain. These special TRAITS offer a **key to the whole story of women.**

Consider this: Because women were either pregnant or nursing and, in general, could not participate with the men in the long grueling hunts, they developed a different set of evolutionary traits based around children, community and a love of the environment. The skills of women were life affirming and their success was measured in the survival of the children.

Some of the traits which are found in the Female brain, included the incredible social bonding skills between women in the community, their nurturing nature, their ability to both show emotions and understand the emotions of others in order to enhance communication, and their tremendous empathy for all of life.

Then, suddenly, about **10,000 years ago**, everything changed. Overnight EVERYTHING changed! That is, almost everything changed!

The one thing that did not change were the differences between MEN and WOMEN that evolved differently in the MALE and FEMALE brain.

For now, the key message, which lies at the heart of the whole story is that these 10 special evolutionary traits, developed in women, just so

ALEXIA PARKS

happen to be the very traits that are needed for leadership of today's volatile, complex, interconnected world.

These 10 TRAITS found the female brain also reflect a profound love of Nature and the Environment. They are life affirming.

__Leadership Lessons__: When you focus on EACH of these 10 special traits – which you already have - when you study them & meditate on each trait, they will manifest as inner power, courage, and a will to lead. Look for opportunities to integrate them into your life at home, work, and school

The Greatest Revolution
In Human History

During the millions of years, known as the Old Stone Age, men and women faced many dangers on a daily basis. Survival was always the first thing on their mind.

Survival and the search for food were linked. So, one could say, the mantra of this age was: **food, food, food**. In fact, if there had been a job listing posted during the Old Stone Age it would have read:

Wanted: One Hunter Gatherer.

While men went out in teams to hunt for food, sometimes on a run of 20 miles or longer, women, of necessity, stayed close to home.

Pregnant or nursing, the job of the women was to ensure the survival of the children, and prepare the meal. These were skills that required great courage, for at any moment, they had to meet the challenges and ever changing circumstances of their environment while the men were off hunting. They also had to continue nursing their babies, whether or not they themselves had enough food to eat.

The tasks required by this division of labor, evolved into 10 traits found the male and female brain. Then, suddenly, in the "blink of an eye," after a long sojourn in the wild lasting millions of years, the Agricultural Revolution began.

As recently as 10,000 years ago, in six "hot spots" around the world, the Agricultural Revolution began, and suddenly, everything changed. And where were those hot spots? They were in China, near Beijing; in India, in the Indus Valley; and in Iraq, in Mesopotamia – the fertile land between the Tigris and Euphrates Rivers. They also included "hot spots" in West Africa, Mexico, and the Andes.

With human settlement in mind, it could be said that the Agricultural Revolution was the greatest revolution in all of human history. It *could be said* that it was *infinitely* greater than the Russian Revolution, the French Revolution and the American Revolution.

Why was it greater than all of these? It was greater, because "overnight," we switched our occupation from the active, nomadic lifestyle of the hunter-gatherer to the more sedentary lifestyle of the farmer and city dweller.

10 TRAITS - LEADERS OF POWER AND COURAGE

The Agricultural Revolution not only included massive cultivation of grain, specifically cereal grains, but also the domestication of many species of animals, including cows, pigs, sheep, and chickens.

For the first time in human history we did not have to go out the next day and look for food. We had as much food as we wanted. We became farmers, and sedentary village and city dwellers, instead of active, nomadic hunter-gatherers.

For the first time in human history, towns and cities arose. For the first time in human history, there was private property.

For the first time in human history, there were massive population explosions in areas where there was an abundance of food. **A tidal wave of change swept over the woman's hearth.**

The nomadic lifestyle was replaced by the life of the farmer, and later, city dweller. Villages grew into towns, and towns into cities.

Overnight, populations rapidly expanded; and as overcrowding pushed greater numbers of people closer together, they became stratified into incredibly complex social structures and hierarchical systems.

For the first time in human history, giant bureaucracies and complex legal

ALEXIA PARKS

systems arose. Bureaucracies and legal systems were built to manage the growing problems of an ever more complex society. There was an explosion of material goods. There was also destruction of the environment.

The very mega-structure of rapidly expanding cities around world, and the complexity of rules and regulations to run them brought an abrupt end to the Old Stone Age.

10 TRAITS - LEADERS OF POWER AND COURAGE

10 MAJOR CHANGES IN *HUMAN LIFESTYLE* FROM THE OLD STONE AGE TO THE AGRICULTURAL REVOLUTION

© *Parks-Rauch Chart of Comparisons*

The Old Stone Age		The Agricultural Revolution
100% Egalitarian & Functional	**Social Structure**	100% Hierarchical Men vs Women
Active Nomadic Hunter-Gatherer	**Lifestyle**	Sedentary Farmer & City Dweller
Scarce	**Food Supply**	Abundance of Grain. The Domestication of Animals and Plants
Around 100 (in small groups worldwide)	**Population Size**	Population Explosion
25 years maximum	**Life Span**	Approximately 75 years
Simple, with few material possessions.	**Complexity**	Abundance. Destruction of the Environment
Lived off the land.	**Land**	Farming, private property, & water rights
None	**Legal System**	Complex
The Woman's Hearth	**Community Development**	The development of cities.
Very Simple	**Social Customs**	Very Complex

ALEXIA PARKS

I think you see the general picture that is emerging here. The stark contrast between the Old Stone Age and the Agricultural Revolution could not have been sharper. Once they became stationary and well fed, those small nomadic groups suddenly burgeoned into the massive populations of modern civilization. They became hierarchical and patriarchal.

Overnight everything changed. That is, *almost everything* changed.

The one thing that did not change, that remains true even today, were the evolutionary traits that were based on survival, that evolved in the brains of men and women over more than a million years.

In general, it takes 100,000 years or longer to change our biology, our genetics, our hardwired brain.

While social customs and social mores are constantly evolving to reflect changing times, traits of men and women have evolved over thousands of years to change.

Because of this, the survival traits that were shaped by evolution in humans in the Old Stone Age are still present in the male and female brain.

Forged in a much simpler world where the division of labor was clearly defined, and based on the specific tasks that each of their jobs demanded, the brains of men and women respond differently to stress.

10 TRAITS - LEADERS OF POWER AND COURAGE

The chart that follows in Part II explains this more fully and includes all of the 10 major evolutionary traits of men and women. For now, a brief overview that touches on some of these traits will give you a general idea of these differences.

For the men, their 10 unique traits enabled them to focus on a single goal: to follow the deer, to hunt as a team, and to draw upon their testosterone driven strength and endurance for the long journey.

Of necessity, the evolutionary traits that were selected out in women included an ability to focus on many things at the same time, and to pay attention to everything in the local environment that supported her and her family, including the plants and animals.

A woman's natural ability to multi-task, and affirm everything that strengthened the health and well being of her children and her community, became part of her survival strategy.

This trait representing a deep love of people, diversity, and community evolved through evolutionary times in the female brain.

In fact, this fact alone is astounding to contemplate, and is so relevant today, that it bears repeating: A major leadership trait found in the female brain is a **deep love of people, diversity, and community.**

ALEXIA PARKS

Even with the dramatic cultural changes brought to humankind by the Agricultural Revolution, nothing has changed this evolutionary hardwiring in men and women. Why? *Because, in general, it takes **100,000 years or more** to change our biology, our genetics, our hardwired brain.*

The only thing that has changed has been the "learned behavior" of men and women based on ever-changing social and cultural customs.

From the perspective of evolutionary psychology, which scientists and anthropologists now use as the basic model from which to study human evolution, there is a tremendous amount of hardwiring in the male and the female brain. Various estimates suggest that **this hardwiring comprises up to 80% of the modern human brain.**

If our brain is already 80% hardwired by evolutionary biology, what do we know about the remaining 20% percent?

The remaining 20% is called the Cortex. Superimposed over our hardwired, fixed brain, is an outer layer of the brain called the cerebral cortex, or "the gray matter."

The most highly developed part of the cerebral cortex is known as the frontal cortex, which does most of human thinking, including abstract thinking. This is the brain that can change. It can grow new brain cells. It is said to be Neuroplastic.

10 TRAITS - LEADERS OF POWER AND COURAGE

What is especially important to the anthropologists, brain scientists, and other professionals who study "learned behavior," is this frontal area: the

frontal cortex because it is the focal point of learned behavior, social conditioning, and what is called "social culture."

So, if the hardwired brain is looked at as *"hardware,"* then the newer part of the brain (the frontal cortex, the "plastic brain") which can adapt, learn new behaviors, and change as cultural rules and mores change, could be called the *"software"* of the brain.

The many different "software programs" used by the brain give it the quality referred to by modern science as **neuroplasticity**. Neuroplasticity refers to the "plastic" brain that can change itself, and can grow new brain cells. It is the hottest topic in brain function research today.

It is this malleable, "plastic" part of the brain which is shaped by 10,000 different cultures in thousands of different ways. It is shaped by our parents, our community, our country, and by religion, culture and customs.

So, the ways in which a person "fits in" to their culture is learned behavior. Because 20% of the brain is malleable, it can learn how to "fit in" to any

culture, or respond to any circumstance through upbringing, education and training. It can also be trained to be submissive or suppressed.

ALEXIA PARKS

For a reference point, consider how a dog is trained to be a family pet. It can be trained for many different behaviors, and respond to many different commands. **However, underneath its learned behavior, is its evolutionary hardwiring**.

In humans, there are an infinite number of ways for the human brain to be "domesticated;" that is, to learn how to adapt and fit in to a culture.

It can also be trained to be submissive. In a 2013 study titled **<u>MEN RULE</u>** - by American University's Women and Politics Institute researchers report that 67% of women have been conditioned to be submissive. They wait for an invitation before taking a leadership action.

However, the good news is that using our neuroplastic brain, we can learn how to "drive" our own body chemistry in any direction we choose in order to strengthen and increase our capacity for success.

What this means, in terms of humans, is that men can condition their neuroplastic brain to become more expressive, to be more collaborative, to become "Mr Mom," and become the primary caretakers of children.

However, while men can learn how to become primary caretakers of children, there is no society in the world where the men are the natural caretakers of children. This is absolute. It is a *learned* behavior.

10 TRAITS - LEADERS OF POWER AND COURAGE

And conversely, women can learn "masculine behavior." They can learn how to "fit in" to masculine structured corporations and political systems. They can all learn how to be rough, tough soldiers.

Women can be trained to kill. They can join men on the hunt. They can become part of a team. They can also learn how to lower the tone of their voice, slow down their speech, and suppress their emotions. However, these are not natural traits of women.

In each case, this would be *learned behavior* as opposed to the different skill sets and traits found in the male and female brain.

Said differently, the social customs of any family, community, country, to culture represent the *conditioned* behavior in men and women.

The hardwired brain is FIXED. It has been shaped by evolutionary biology over human history, and as stated, it can can take as long as 100,000 years or longer to change.

What lurks below the surface of our socially conditioned neuroplastic brain is our hardwired brain. In addition, *the differences* between the constellation of 10 traits found in the male and 10 traits found in the female brain - activated in times of great stress - makes all the difference in the world.

In fact, there is no other way to approach the human condition, and the

ALEXIA PARKS

future of life on Earth, but to understand the significance of this constellation of 10 traits, and what happens when the male, or female brain is activated in times of GREAT stress. What difference do these differences make?

To see this big picture, one has to go beyond relationships, the workplace, politics, economics, healthcare, and the environment. The big picture necessitates pulling from hard sciences such as medicine and evolutionary

biology, and the soft sciences including sociology, psychology, and both cultural and physical anthropology.

We humans are the descendants of hearty Stone Age survivors. Over those millions of years, the men and women who "got it right" were able to survive long enough to produce the next generation. They became our ancient ancestors.

Because the Agricultural Revolution happened only 10,000 years ago – long after the hardwiring in our brain was fixed – it is easy to forget that *the abundance of food*, especially grains, brought to us by the Agricultural Revolution was the starting point for complex challenges facing us today.

These complexities - these multiple stress points - impact our neuroplastic brain . When they overwhelm our neuroplastic, "conditioned" brain, they trigger TRAITS that lie underneath the surface of the Cortex, in our hardwired "fixed" brain.

10 TRAITS - LEADERS OF POWER AND COURAGE

Under great stress, 10 traits found in the male and female brain override our conditioned brain and drive our behavior.

Men's unique traits have led us through the Ages of War. Their innovations and technological solutions have brought us this far. And we have them to thank for this leadership.

However, in today's IDEA Economy, also known as the "Thank You" Economy and the "Service Economy," the FEMALE brain is uniquely suited to manage these high levels of stress and complexity with confidence.

Today's world needs more collaboration and nurturing. That's why as countries begin to rise up the economic index of development, these natural leadership traits, found in the female brain are well suited for governance of cooperative, collaborative, sustainable societies, in dynamic synergy with men.

**Leadership Lessons**: For men and women, our hardwired brain is activated when there is discord, aggression, or conflict. It reveals itself when there is fear, a threat, or when "a target of concern" comes into view. It is why men and women react differently when placed under stress; and why more women are needed at the decision-making table, in a dynamic partnership with men. In volatile times, the social, empathetic, diplomatic skills of women can play a key role in decision-making, reducing risk, and leadership.

10 Major Leadership Traits

In the chart that follows, we intentionally summarized a *huge amount of data* from major fields that all converge on the same thesis and that is:

That the very traits that were selected out by Mother Nature, that are found in the female brain, are ironically the very traits that are needed in leadership today at all levels of society.

I like to say that these are traits that are needed, urgently needed, in the world today to manage the complexities of today's volatile, complex, interconnected world. There is no right or wrong. In terms of evolutionary biology, necessity is the Mother of Invention. This is how it works.

In this case, Mother Nature, through evolutionary biology, has selected out certain traits for human survival itself. And the difference in these special traits - that make up 80% of the evolutionary wiring of the male and female brain - show up in the way we respond to events at home, in the workplace, and how we think about the environment.

Today, if you add in the complexities and problems related to climate change, the issue humans face today, is *human survival*, on a global scale.

10 TRAITS - LEADERS OF POWER AND COURAGE

And the issue of human survival now extends beyond the woman's community to the community of nations around the globe.

Our interconnected relationships and alliances – which shape our neuroplastic brain - now include the whole world and its 10,000 different cultures.

I like to put it this way: the skills found in the male brain have brought us this far: through the ages of exploration, empire building and war. Now, the leadership traits that are urgently needed today to manage the complexities of our volatile world and to shift the focus to sustainability, can be found in the female brain.

How many women are needed in leadership in dynamic synergy with men at ALL levels of society?

Enough to make the difference!

ALEXIA PARKS

So, take a minute and look at the following list and see if you agree with me that the following leadership traits are what the world needs now in our leaders.

1. Social bonding that includes diverse cultures
2. The ability to freely express emotions, as well as understand and respond to the emotional needs of others.
4. Empathy for others.
5. The ability to easily display affections.
6. A love of people and community
7. Multi-tasking skills at many levels, simultaneously
8. Acute awareness of, and a love of, the environment.
9. Success at balancing many different competing factors.
10. Great diplomatic, negotiating, and problem-solving skills. Skilled at decision-making, with the ability to befriend adversaries and create win-win situations.

10 TRAITS - LEADERS OF POWER AND COURAGE

10 MAJOR TRAITS THE MALE AND FEMALE BRAIN © Parks-Rauch - The Chart of Opposites		
Male Traits	**TRAITS**	**Female Traits**
Teamwork	**Social Mind**	Social Networking
Testosterone Driven. Aggressive. Strength & Endurance. Muscle and Bone Density	**Hormones**	Estrogen, Oxytocin, Bonding. Stored fat that converts to milk when nursing.
Suppresses emotions.	**Emotions**	Readily Displays Emotions; Easily reads the emotions of others.
Low Levels of Empathy	**Empathy**	Highly Empathetic
Harder for men to touch.	**Touch**	Displays touch and affection easily
Love of machines, tools & technology.	**Primary Love**	Love of people and community
Focused Concentration	**Goal Setting**	Multi-Tasking
Lower	**Fine Point Discrimination**	Higher
Lower	**Balancing Many Factors Simultaneously**	Higher
Fight or Flight	**Facing Danger**	Tend & Befriend

ALEXIA PARKS

<u>NOTES</u>

1 THE COLLABORATIVE LEADER

The social mind of the testosterone-driven male brain is based on teamwork.

To be on a team requires that everyone on that team be tuned into the same "radio station," that is, the same wavelength. The team must share a common language that is mutually understandable and precise. Everyone on the team must stay focused on a common goal.

With this in mind, remember that the work of the men of the Old Stone Age was that of the hunter, and **men hunted as a team**. Their common goal, on a daily basis, was to stay focused on food: to follow the food, to hunt down the prey, then kill it and carry it back to the village.

This long distance hunt that covered many miles, and could last for several days, required strength, stamina, and aggression by the men. It also required long periods of social isolation, risk-taking, and an ever-present risk of injury, broken bones, and pain and suffering.

In short, it required that men learn to suppress their emotions for the greater good of the team. It also required that they kill without empathy. They had to put their body in harm's way, close enough to look the animal in the eye and think: "You are food," because they knew that food was survival itself.

This constellation of characteristics and skills, selected out over human history by evolutionary biology, paints a picture of the condition of men that required their teamwork, competition, and the ability to focus on a single goal with no distractions. These traits shaped the social mind of men.

The social mind of women is based on social networking.
In contrast to men, the story of women from the dawn of human history to modern times, evolved in community and at the hearth. Because of this, the social mind of the female brain evolved in a way that was the very opposite of traits found in the male brain. Like Stone Age woman from PALEO times, the social mind of today's modern women is able to understand the unmet, unspoken needs of others, and freely express emotions.

Women, one could say, are skilled at social communication to the benefit of the larger community.

10 TRAITS - LEADERS OF POWER AND COURAGE

The focus of the female brain is on sustaining life. Due to their ability to give birth, and breastfeed their young, this has been the job of women throughout human history. The female brain is life affirming and focused on the well being of others.

Over millennia, the skills associated with ensuring the well-being of their children, enhanced women's social networking skills. It also shaped their ability to interact with, collaborate with others, and balance out the diverse interests of others for the common good of all. Through evolutionary psychology, these are the skill sets and traits found in the female brain.

This fact, affirmed by research in the field of evolutionary biology and evolutionary psychology , is important to emphasize and restate.

Women are able to *communicate* their emotions more freely than men, because their brain has been shaped by evolution to be empathetic - both verbal and non-verbal - to easily read other people's emotions, and to intuit the unspoken needs of others.

Because this trait, found the female brain, is focused on the greater good of the community, especially the well-being of children, women are constantly bonding on every level.

Today we know that a lot of communication is based on emotional intelligence. About 80% of all decision-making of both men and women, is based

ALEXIA PARKS

on their emotional response. This trait has been selected out through our human history and found in the female brain, because it is the "social" glue that has enabled women to bond with members of their community for the purpose of raising children.

What women have known throughout our evolutionary history, that is still true today is this: "It takes a village to raise a child."

The women's community around the fire in the Old Stone Age has now become a "community of nations" and our needs are intertwined.

Today, however, the interconnected nature of cultures around the world, linked together 24/7 by economic needs and modern communications technologies, places uncommon stress on our hardwired brain. It becomes activated. Engaged. Decision-making under stress can have global impacts.

This moment-by-moment engagement from the standpoint of leaders and policy makers **represents a whole new opportunity for women as leaders**, in our whole new, interconnected world. Under stress, the 10 traits found in the female brain shift from "fight or flight" to diplomacy.

Today, if anyone takes a course in cultural anthropology, they will learn that there are over 100 groups that are marginal around the world that still live in the Old Stone Age. So by studying those 100 groups around the world, anthropologists are really looking at humans before we made the transition into

10 TRAITS - LEADERS OF POWER AND COURAGE

the Agricultural Revolution. It offers a look back at the dawn of human history, from whence we came. The complexity of modern times, offers a hint at where we are heading.

Since the dawn of human history, the social mind of women, has been uniquely suited to manage high levels of complexity. It is our heritage and a key trait that we bring to modern times.

Leadership Lessons: *When you learn about your social mind, study it, and meditate on it, you will then discover its many benefits for your life. To exercise your social mind, look for opportunities to network, to stand up and speak up about issues that matter most to you.*

ALEXIA PARKS

NOTES

2 THE NURTURING LEADER

Men & Testosterone.

When a baby is born, it is held up, and the first question that is usually asked is: Is it a boy or girl? This is called the **primary** sexual characteristic, and it is very obvious.

However, the major difference between boys and girls in adolescence is the hormone Testosterone. Testosterone is what makes little boys, boys.

What are some of those **secondary** sexual characteristics of Testosterone in boys and men? They include denser muscles, denser bones, more risk-taking behavior, more aggressive behavior than women, and the ability to suppress emotions.

ALEXIA PARKS

In short, Testosterone is the perfect hormone for the rigor and endurance demanded in a long distant hunt by a team of men.

The hormone Testosterone, in fact, actually changes the structure, or hard-wiring, of the male brain to be more aggressive and more risk-taking.

Women and Estrogen:

By contrast, what makes little girls, girls, is the hormone Estrogen. And what are some of the **secondary** characteristics of Estrogen? It isn't dense muscles and bone. Instead it is a much greater percentage of body fat both in the hip area, and the women's breasts.

Why does Estrogen drive so much more body fat in women than in men?

The function of body fat in women, which developed over hundreds of thousands of years, was *to ensure the survival of the nursing baby*. The body fat in women was carried as stored calories for the baby, when there wasn't enough food for the woman to eat.

10 TRAITS - LEADERS OF POWER AND COURAGE

This stored fat was converted into breast milk for the nursing baby. The hormone, Estrogen, that facilitates this conversion, is hardwired into a woman's hormonal system by Mother Nature. It acted like an insurance policy to make sure that there would be enough food for the baby, when food was scarce.

So, women who have muscles and bones that are not as dense as men, have instead, a much higher percentage of body fat. In medical anthropology, for example, **the large buttocks of women of childbearing age**, even in petite women, is referred to as steatopygia.

Steatopygia means the storage of calories in the buttocks area, because those calories of fat can be translated into milk for the baby during lean times. In modern times, it might be a sign that a person has eaten too many *refined* carbohydrates, or is pre-diabetic.

In evolutionary terms, the large buttocks represents a symbol of fertility to a man. He may think: "If I mate with her, she will have enough food to feed my child."

ALEXIA PARKS

Along with a higher percentage of body fat, the hormone Estrogen in women also means that they will have higher voices, and no facial hair.

However, perhaps the most important characteristic, in light of the subject of this book is this: **Lacking significant amounts of the Testosterone hormone, women are less aggressive than men, and better at social bonding.**

Women and Oxytocin

The hormone Oxytocin is basically known as the bonding hormone. The strongest bond in humans is the mother-baby bond. The maternal bond is cemented by the hormone Oxytocin.

Oxytocin, also hardwired into a woman's hormonal system by Mother Nature, is released from the master gland, the pituitary gland in the mother's brain, as soon as a baby suckles. A neuronal reflex in her brain will release it. The first time the baby goes for the breast milk, the hormone Oxytocin is released for the bonding of the baby with the mother.

10 TRAITS - LEADERS OF POWER AND COURAGE

Through the hormone Oxytocin, women are chemically bonded with their children, and by extension, with their family and their community.

For men, in general, bonding with their children is more of *a learned behavior,* through upbringing, education, parenting, and social customs.

The significance of this fact and other evolutionary differences between men and women cannot be emphasized enough. Why?

These differences relate to every single human being on the planet. They show up in the way we respond to relationships, the workplace, to politics, to economics, to the environment, to raising children, to adolescents, to marriage, and about 100 other major topics.

In the Chart of Opposites - we intentionally summarized huge amounts of data from major fields that all converge on the same thesis. And this is that *the very traits* that were selected out by Mother Nature for women *are, ironically* the very traits that are needed in the world today today to shift the world from economies based on overconsumption, competition, and conflict to those based on collaboration, cooperation, and sustainability.

In short, the attributes that evolved through evolutionary biology in the human brain relate to every single human endeavor in the world today.

There is no right or wrong. It's not that men are better than women, or women better than men. The traits of both men and women were selected, by necessity, for survival itself, and are found in the male and female brain.

The skills of men have brought us this far. Now, it's as if Mother Nature herself is calling out to the FEMALE brain, asking us to stand up, speak up, to take a seat at the decision-making table, in dynamic synergy with men.

So, if the real bottom line is: "human survival," there needs to be a quantum shift toward *women in leadership roles* at all levels of society. How many? Enough to make the difference.

Leadership Lessons: *When you learn about the human bonding hormone Oxytocin, study it, and meditate on its power, then look for opportunities to reach out to others, to connect through the healing power of touch, or a helping hand.*

3 EXPRESSIVE LEADER

Because women were relegated to the hearth, and childrearing for most of human history, a women's emotional brain is bigger and better developed, than a man's emotional brain. The emotional brain is also referred to as the limbic system.

The reason for its larger size in women is due to evolutionary biology. For over 99.9% of human history, the job of women was to bond, not only with their children, and the animals that lived with them, but *to also bond and interact with other women.*

This emotional bonding helped ensure a social network of support from other women in the community.

ALEXIA PARKS

In the Old Stone Age, the HEART of the women's hearth was the group of socially connected women, their children, their animals, and the simple tools they used for cooking and meal preparation.

This natural form of emotional communication ensured their survival. Today it is referred to as emotional intelligence and is a key leadership skill. Know thyself. Develop a knowledge of others, and an awareness of the outer world and its relationship to you.

Women excel at emotional intelligence. A women's emotional skills include both the ability to freely express emotions, and also read the emotions of others, both verbal and non-verbal.

Remember that old cliché, "a woman's intuition"? This refers to her ability to read the emotions of others. It is a key benefit gained from the woman's larger emotional brain. Her brain evolved over history to be expressive.

By contrast, the smaller emotional male brain was selected out as an essential trait for the male brain, through evolutionary biology. Why?

10 TRAITS - LEADERS OF POWER AND COURAGE

It gave men the ability to *suppress* their emotions when out on the hunt, and to make a kill - perhaps with their bare hands.. The ability to suppress emotions is not a learned behavior; it evolved over history in the male brain.

To emphasize this point: over thousands of years, driven by the incredible pressure of the long distance hunt, those Stone Age men who were able to suppress their emotions became valued members of the hunting team.

The physically demanding tasks of the hunt, required men who were able to suppress their emotions when injured, or in pain.

Evolution selected out men who could suppress their fear when attacked by an animal, or when they were participating in a kill.

Men hunting together in a team knew that if they showed any emotions, or any feelings at all, this display of emotions would be perceived as a sign of weakness.

For the success of the team, there could be no weak link to distract them, or slow them down on their long distance hunt. The demands of their job meant that they could not be distracted by pain, suffering, or fear.

Because of this evolutionary suppression of emotions by men, the way they communicate is a lot more intellectual, unemotional, or left brain logical.

Men learned to suppress any stirrings of the emotional brain for the greater good of the team while out on the hunt, and to show strength for the kill.

By contrast, women learned to express their emotions for the greater good of their social network, for community bonding, and for child rearing. Over time, this ability to freely express their emotions shaped the female brain.

Leadership Lessons: *How you communicate and present yourself is a very personal, spontaneous, natural process for you.* Effective communications *takes discipline and focus. Each word, like body language, has an impact.*

4 THE EMPATHETIC LEADER

The emotional brain of women makes it easy for a woman to read the emotions of her children, the animals around the hearth, and to read the emotions of other people on both a verbal and non-verbal level.

The female brain has to be able to quickly understand the emotional needs of those who are not able to fully communicate them.

Another name for this trait is empathy.

The corresponding "low empathy" trait in the male brain would be part of the same constellation of traits that gave them the ability to suppress emotions for the long distance hunt, and the ability to kill animals for the welfare of their family, and even, in times of war and warfare, to kill other humans.

In general, when a man sees someone who is sad, it may not affect him the same way as a woman, because his male brain has evolved to suppress emotions. His brain has been shaped throughout evolutionary history to be part of a team. Coupled with the hormone, testosterone, it can drive men to become competitive, aggressive, and territorial.

In general, lower levels of empathy may explain why some men don't like spending time trying to understand, express, or empathize with the unstated needs of teammates, co-workers, or family. Less expressive, this trait enabled men to focus instead on a single goal, with no distractions.

With women, it's just the opposite. Evolution has shaped the female brain to be emotional and expressive to ensure the survival of their children and community.

Leadership Lessons: *A woman's natural ability to be empathetic, or compassionate, or to express compassion for life – all life on Earth – draws people together like a gravitational force, for the common good.*

5 THE HEALING POWER OF TOUCH

Another characteristic of the emotional brain of women is their constant touching and nurturing of children, friends and community. This trait is found in the female brain for social bonding, and it helps unite the community.

Could this unique trait of women also form the basis for developing peaceful, cooperative societies? Consider the following:

Most people know the name Jane Goodall. Goodall is well known for her work with chimpanzees in Tanzania. Staring in 1977, she documented that chimps in the wild are are patriarchal aggressive, and territorial.

ALEXIA PARKS

By contrast, **few people know about another species** - which separated from the "Goodall chimps" to follow a different evolutionary path, about a million years ago. The **Bonobos** are matriarchal, cooperative, and peaceful.

The matriarchal Bonobos will spend the whole day constantly grooming, and touching, for the greater good of social bonding in the community. The Bonobos use touching, hugging, and "dancing" in a group to elevate the social bonding of their community.

And BOTH the **Chimps and the Bonobos** shares 99.5% of the same DNA as humans, in the same sequence.

Why is this is important? Because to me, the Bonobos represent the greatest experiment of all time, taking place right now in Nature - of a cooperative, peaceful, matriarchal society that has remained that way for more than a million years. **The Bonobos remind** us that *Peace on Earth* is possible.

It's also important for another reason. Like the matriarchal BONOBOS, the constellation of 10 special TRAITS found the female brain just so happen to be **the very opposite** - the complementary, synergistic, opposite - of those traits found in the male brain.

10 TRAITS - LEADERS OF POWER AND COURAGE

There is no right or wrong. It's not that women are better than men, or that men are better than women. It's just that our BRAINS evolved differently for different tasks over our evolutionary history.

Like chimps in the wild, the male brain has been shaped by evolution to be aggressive, competitive and territorial. By contrast, the maternal female brain has evolved to be more social, empathetic, and diplomatic.

These differences show up in the way women respond at home, work or school. They show up in the way women think about economics, politics and the environment. They control how we raise our children, how we treat our friends, and how we resolve conflicts.

The male brain has been "grooved" through the "loneliness of the long distance hunt," to suppress emotions, empathy, and touch. When men do touch, it is all to often very superficial and ritualistic. In western cultures, in particular, a strong handshake between men will suffice.In addition, there is a phenomenon called homophobia, the fear or hatred of homosexuals. This fear reinforces the pre-existing, long standing taboo of touch in men, and makes casual physical contact with each other more difficult.

Leadership Lessons: The Bonobos represent the greatest experiment of all time, taking place *right now* in Nature, of a cooperative, matriarchal, and peaceful society. The Bonobos show that lasting *Peace on Earth* is possible.

ALEXIA PARKS

NOTES

6 COMPASSIONATE LEADERSHIP

Men love their motorcycles. Men love their cars. Men who go to war, have been known to paint symbolic images of women on their weapons, and give them a women's name.

Men are known for their love of machines, tools and technology.
It could be said that the primary love of men is inanimate, dead objects: tool making, tools, and technology.

By contrast, women have a love of people, diversity and community.

And scientifically speaking, this is true. Researchers at Cambridge and the University College of London's School of Economics have done extensive research in this area on both women and men.

ALEXIA PARKS

The term these researchers use to describe a man's love of tools, technology and tool-making, that is shaped by evolutionary biology into their brain is: "systematic thinkers."

A primary love of people and community is found in the mental ("mentalistic") sphere of the female brain. It stands in stark contrast to the "systematic thinking" the male brain. Research studies and everyday observation confirm this finding.

From the Old Stone Age up to modern times, men have been, and continue to be systematic thinkers. Their orientation is toward dead, inanimate objects meaning that they love machines, technology and tools that they can take apart and put together again. This primary love of men is their love of technology, and a love of trying to figure out how things work.

Because of this trait, society owe a debt of gratitude to men. Their teamwork, single pointed focus, and their skills have brought us this far. The leadership of men has brought us to where we are today, and we have prospered.

10 TRAITS - LEADERS OF POWER AND COURAGE

However, in today's interconnected, complex world, the challenges that lie ahead for successful leaders require the use of a different set of skills. These challenges require a shift of focus to the female brain; that is, to a whole new kind of leadership based on the female brain; with a clear understanding of how the female brain actually works!

Some would call this moment in human history a tipping point, a watershed moment. The complexity of today's world demands that more attention be paid to ALL life on Earth. It demands that we focus on solutions that are people oriented, community oriented, life sustaining, and life affirming.

Could it be that we as a human species have come full circle, and that today, we are at the same crisis point that humankind faced in the Old Stone Age? Survival itself? Do today's women feel an intuitive need - an urge perhaps driven by necessity to lead the way forward, in dynamic synergy with men.

Leadership Lessons: *When you learn about your natural love of people, diversity and community, its many benefits will enhance your life, and offer new opportunities to express this primary love, in community.*

ALEXIA PARKS

NOTES

7   **THE MINDFUL LEADER**

In looking at the trait of goal setting, let's focus on men first, and their skill of one-pointed, focused concentration.

Remember that we spoke earlier about the evolutionary pressure on men to become part of a long distance testosterone-driven team?

The goal for each man, and collectively as a team, was a simple one. They had to bring back food to the women and children, which sustained life itself. There was no margin of error. The main trait that men developed through teamwork, was incredible focus and concentration.

Men became skilled at cybernetic goal setting, focusing with one pointed concentration on their goal, just like a cruise missile or drone will zig and zag until it converges on the target.

So men, compared to women, do not like distractions. Men function best when there is a single focus, a clear-cut, affirmative goal, and the use of a common language to keep them on the same wavelength.

This intense focus is also seen in the traditional, male dominated corporate world, as employees are trained to work in teams and focus on achieving a single goal. It also shows up in extreme conditions such as war, and is reinforced through the training of soldiers and military personnel around the world.

By contrast, the 10 traits of women noted here are <u>almost diametrically opposite</u> to those of men. And it is easy to see why those traits are urgently needed in leadership roles today to help manage our complex, volatile world.

Over our human history, because of the very nature of a nomadic lifestyle, and later at home and hearth in villages and towns, women had to balance out many competing demands at the same time. Women had to focus on the

10 TRAITS - LEADERS OF POWER AND COURAGE

demands of the children, the animals, the meal preparation and cooking, the gathering of local herbs and plants, along with many other tasks, simultaneously.

Today this is roughly synonymous with what we call multi-tasking. The male brain has evolved to focus on one goal, one objective. **The female brain has been shaped by evolution to be able to balance many goals, simultaneously.**

And the startling fact is this. Brain studies show that the connection between the two brain hemispheres, left and right, is more developed in the female brain.

This more developed connection, called "The Bridge of Consciousness" or Corpus Callosum, has been enhanced in the female brain over human history for multi-tasking and balancing out many factors.

<u>**Leadership Lessons**</u>: *When you learn about your natural born ability to set goals, and manage goals successfully, simultaneously, you may want to set even higher goals for yourself. Free of outer distractions, you can learn to use your own neuroplastic brain to drive your body chemistry in any direction you choose, to strengthen and increase your capacity for success. If this thought overwhelms you, ask me. I can show you how to do this.*

ALEXIA PARKS

NOTES

8 ENVIRONMENTAL LEADERSHIP

Because of the local food gathering skills of women of the Old Stone Age, including their ability to gather nuts and seeds, and to know which trees bore edible fruit and when it would ripen, the female brain evolved with fine point discrimination. It became a repository of critical, life-affirming knowledge.

Thus the term Fine Point Discrimination refers to a woman's keen ability to be able to dissect out the various species of plants, seeds, herbs, and colors, around the hearth, or home for use by the family and community.

It refers to a woman's ability to see *both* the forest AND the trees. Her deep love of the environment and its distinguishing elements. both the parts and the whole.

ALEXIA PARKS

Interestingly, the hottest new theory in cultural anthropology is that the origin of the Agricultural Revolution belongs to seed gathering women, that seeds for used in food preparation could also be planted, and ultimately harvested.

Again, it is worth remembering that in hunter-gatherer times, because women were either pregnant or nursing, they were relegated to the camp site or the hearth. They could not leave nursing, and the children behind in order to hunt with the men. So, in addition, to raising children and animals, a great amount of their time was spent becoming experts of local flora and fauna.

Because of this role in gathering food from around the hearth, women's brains are better at determining which plants are edible and which are to be avoided; which herbs are medicinal and beneficial as botanicals. This trait was shaped by evolution in the female brain.

The male brain, on the other hand, is just the opposite. Throughout human history, men were able to focus on a single goal with no distractions. Because their job was to hunt for food, men developed the skills necessary for a total focus on the target. And the target, of course, was the object of the hunt.

10 TRAITS - LEADERS OF POWER AND COURAGE

The result is that the male brain is much better at cybernetic goal setting and keeping everyone focused on achieving a common goal.

By contrast, the female brain in a multi-sensory environment, is much better at detecting subtleties of colors, shapes, and textures: seeing the whole and the parts simultaneously. This is why women over our human history have remained a repository of critical, life-affirming information.

Today, with the global challenge of climate change, we are reminded that the HOPE for the future lies in - both men and women - step into Environmental Leadership roles in dynamic synergy with Mother Nature.

Leadership Lessons: *When you learn about your Fine Point trait and focus on it through a series of daily habits,. it will manifest as a deep love of the environment and a will to protect Planet Earth.*

ALEXIA PARKS

NOTES

9 THE BALANCING & PRIORITIZING LEADER

Because of the relegation of women to the hearth, where many things were occurring at many levels, simultaneously, one of the major evolutionary traits found in women is their ability to balance out many competing factors, in real time.

The woman's brain has been neurologically wired to balance out everything and prioritize at the same time.

So, for example, women were able to balance out the attention of the children, the family, the needs of the animals, the bonding with other women in the community, and at the same time, attend to the necessities of the hearth in terms of food preparation, and gathering local seeds, herbs and plants.

By contrast, men did not need to learn how to balance out many things at the same time. With one pointed focus, everything else was viewed as a distraction.

Men learned to be successful at ignoring anything that distracted them from the goal. The male brain became skilled at focusing on the cybernetic goal they had selected, and to mentally discard any extraneous factors. As mentioned earlier, these factors might include the distractions of pain, suffering, emotions, hunger, or thirst that they or others might feel, while engaged in a long distance hunt.

Leadership Lessons: *When you learn about your natural ability to balance and prioritize, you will discover its many benefits for your life. A leader learns how to delegate tasks, then manage others to keep them focused on a common goal.*

10 THE DIPLOMATIC LEADER

We've all heard of the **"flight or fight"** response of men when faced with danger. Men, supported by testosterone, strong muscles and dense bones, will quickly assess the situation and then make a quick calculation. They will either stay to fight, and hopefully win, or run away from the situation. They will slay the saber tooth tiger, or run from it. They will fire the weapon, push the button, or wait.

The scientific term for women's response to danger is **"tend and befriend."** Women will move toward danger, not away from it. What is the reason for this, and *why* is it an evolutionary trait of women to befriend danger?

ALEXIA PARKS

Imagine the plight of a 20-year-old Stone Age mother.

Through extensive research, anthropologists believe that because women of the Old Stone Age were either pregnant, nursing, and had children at their feet. When danger approached, a woman could *not* grab her children, the baby in her belly, and the baby at her breast and run from danger. Instead she had to develop a different strategy.

Today some people might call that strategy "diplomacy."

This inability of pregnant,or nursing women, with children at her feet to run away from danger shaped an opposite response that was HARDWIRED in the female brain. Thus, when facing danger, women would tend to negotiate, to "tend and befriend," and to try to work things out.

In short, when a woman is confronted with a level of danger that places GREAT stress on her, her hardwired leadership traits are activated! They are brought to bear on the situation, whether at home, at work, or school. That's why I remind that during complex times: "When the going

10 TRAITS - LEADERS OF POWER AND COURAGE

gets tough, the FEMALE brain turns on."

This is not learned behavior. This skill at defusing conflict, called "tend and befriend," and diplomacy, is **one of a constellation of traits found** in the female brain. It was selected out over hundreds of thousands of years of living out in the wild, out in Mother Nature, where survival was always on a woman's mind.

Those Stone Age women who became skilled in "applied" diplomacy, survived to became our ancient ancestors.

Leadership Lessons: *When you practice this KEY trait, found in the female brain, it will manifest as personal inner power and courage. As a leader, you lead first with deep listening to discover the root cause of the problem, then, act with diplomacy to defuse a conflict. This should be your first option.*

ALEXIA PARKS

WHAT THE WORLD NEEDS NOW

Biology Drives Everything. Everything is basically biologically driven. Eighty percent of our brain is hardwired and lies just below the surface of our learned behavior. This is who we really are.

Today, the skills that are needed in leadership roles at all levels of society are those that are able to multi-task, in real time. To be able to balance out many competing interests, in real time.

It is not just one goal, one target, one direction, and endless wars to win. It's no longer about winners and losers. And it's all happening simultaneously.

In this new emerging world the question is: How can we let everyone win? How can we manage this complexity so that everyone benefits? The skill

10 TRAITS - LEADERS OF POWER AND COURAGE

sets and special traits that are needed to manage this level of complexity in today's volatile world belong to the FEMALE brain.

The origin of women's leadership skills were forged at the hearth over hundreds of thousands of years.

The original children around her Stone Age hearth are now the children of the world. We now live in a "global village."

The animals she tended and the local plants she gathered around the hearth have now become the animals and ecology of the world. Our world is interconnected.

A woman's community in the Old Stone Age has now become a community of nations, and our needs are intertwined.

Today, the very qualities that were shaped by evolutionary necessity - for survival itself - in a woman's brain and in the hormones she was endowed

ALEXIA PARKS

with by Mother Nature, provide the very basis for the 10 TRAITS needed to manage the complexities of our socially networked, volatile world.

Why are the 10 traits found in the female brain needed to manage the growing problems of our interconnected world?

- Because the female brain is life affirming

- The female brain is able to freely express emotions

- It intuits the healing power of touch

- The female brain has fine point discrimination. Using it, we can see the forest and the trees. It enables a deep love of the environment

- The focus of leadership based on the female brain, would shift toward people, diversity and community. Like parenting, the filter that the female brain would bring to the decision-making table and policy-making would be this:

Does this action, this technology, or this proposal protect, sustain, and affirm life? Is it beneficial to all?

Today, the original hearth of women has become the hearth of the world. The Earth and all life on it is now her home. Now is the time for women to lead the way forward.

10 TRAITS - LEADERS OF POWER AND COURAGE

10 MAJOR LEADERSHIP TRAITS

© Parks-Rauch Leadership Chart

RATE YOUR HARDWIRED LEADERSHIP SKILLS

	TRAIT *10 = Highly Skilled*	1	2	3	4	5	6	7	8	9	10	**SCORE**
1	Collaborative											
2	Nurturing											
3	Expressive											
4	Empathetic											
5	Power of Touch											
6	Compassionate											
7	Multi-Tasking											
8	Detects Subtleties											
9	Balance & Prioritize											
10	Diplomacy											
	Your Score											

ALEXIA PARKS

NOTES

10 TRAITS - LEADERS OF POWER AND COURAGE

<u>JUST DO THIS!</u>

Mother Nature's original operating system has now been morphed by modern circumstances to serve a higher purpose. In today's world, what is our higher purpose? How shall we live?

IT WAS a snowy day in winter - A Historic SNOWSTORM the news headlines were calling it - that would shutdown all roads and all tunnels leading into the city. It was a moment, wrote one reporter: "... when "all LIFE stopped."

Or did it?

What if you were given a day off from life as you knew it - ONE PERFECT DAY - to do exactly what YOU wanted to do. What if, on that day, you were offered the chance to live your life YOUR WAY?

What if you were given the chance to live free of all obligations to others; free of other people's expectations? What would you choose to do? What would motivate you to get out of bed that morning? What would put a SMILE on your face? How would you ACT? How would you FEEL?

AND, would you be thankful? Even joyful? Would your heart be filled to the brim with happiness *if you were given a* **REWARD** each time you took the time to <u>**DO THIS**</u> **one thing** first?

Here's what happened when a lawyer, a teacher, and a reporter for a small town newspaper were each given the opportunity to **DO THIS**. Can you tell which one did it, and got the **REWARD**?

In a small town there were three people who were all considered *successful* by anybody's standards. They all lived in nice houses, drove nice cars, and had enough income to buy what they wanted to eat, to dress well, and live "the good life."

The lawyer was well known for his wisdom and for the circle of famous men and women who often called, or stopped by to talk to him. He found it easy to offer a smile and a hug to others. The educator too, was well known. She was known for her frequent "calls to action" sent out to her large network of friends, inviting them to join her at some local protest that she firmly believed would help make the world a better place. And the small town reporter? He was always on edge, always telling others "I gotta run! It's chop-chop time!

Who was the happiest: the lawyer, the educator, or the small town reporter?

10 TRAITS - LEADERS OF POWER AND COURAGE

The lawyer, when asked would say: "There's no more JOY in my life. The educator would complain: "I didn't choose to come into this world of suffering..." and the small town reporter? "I'm living the good life!"

What was the reporter DOING that made the difference?

He was following Mother Nature's **#1 SUCCESS strategy**. Some call it the Prosperity Principle. It started with a feeling of discomfort that led him to this simple, easy to understand rule:

DO THE RIGHT THING.

That's it?

YES! When you DO THE RIGHT THING, Mother Nature gives you a reward. She replaces your sense of edginess with a GOOD FEELING. You feel good. You might even say: "I'm feeling *really good right now*!" It's that simple. Each and every time you do something right, you get a reward. It comes from the INSIDE out.

Some people refer to it as "that feel good" feeling in the belly that makes them want to smile, dance, laugh out loud.

So what did they do to feel THAT good?

ALEXIA PARKS

They did the right thing. They did a RIGHT action, they took a step in the right direction.

Think about it. What do chipmunks, squirrels, and birds have in common? Each day, they have a burning desire, some might call it "driven by hunger," let's call it MOTIVATION, they feel motivated to get up and go outside to search for food. When they find it they get a reward.

So is the reward FOOD? Not exactly. The reward is that "good feeling" inside the chipmunk, squirrel, and bird, that reminds them they did the right thing. The food is what they eat.

We HUMANS get that very same feeling inside of us! It's part of a two step reward system that Mother Nature designed to help animals and humans do the right thing, for SURVIVAL itself!

In the medical journals it's called the Dopamine Serotonin REWARD System, Here's how it works:

In order to ensure that we would survive difficult times outdoors in Nature, Mother Nature gave us a "pharmacy" inside our own body. I guess you could call it a carrot and a stick reward system. To motivate us to DO THE RIGHT THING, she gave us a jolt of dopamine that made us edgy and uncomfortable. It reminded us to get UP, stand up, move our body, do something, anything, that is:

10 TRAITS - LEADERS OF POWER AND COURAGE

LIFE ENHANCING. LIFE AFFIRMING. Or something that has a higher purpose.

That *EDGY* feeling is the first clue that we are on track to getting a REWARD.

So what do we do next?

1. Do we go to the refrigerator and look for the box with that left over birthday cake from last night?

2. Do we call up the pizza place and ask for home delivery?

3. Do we "light up," drink up," doll ourselves up to look like a tempting cupcake for someone else's desire?

OR, do we DO THE RIGHT THING?

Get up, stand up, move our body, breath a little deeper, do some act of compassion, driven by a sense of higher purpose, that returns us - in that moment - to the time when we all lived a PALEO LIFESTYLE without ego, without a separation from Nature, from all that nourished and sustained us surrounding us.

CAUTION: While millions of people have discovered how to follow this simple instruction to success, many other people don't really understand the TRUE meaning of the statement: DO THE RIGHT

THING. So, like the lawyer and the teacher, they reach OUTSIDE of themselves to gain an "off the shelf" reward that brings them a *feel good* EMPTY reward. Yes, the serotonin will flow and make you feel good for a moment, however, there is *nothing life enhancing in the action you took in order to gain the reward.*

This Serotonin pulse that was part of Mother Nature's original operating system has now been morphed by modern circumstances to serve a higher purpose. <u>You can use this same REWARD system to serve a higher cause,</u> tap into your full potential, or maybe be part of millions of right actions of a life fully lived on Purpose. <u>When you transform yourself, you transform the world.</u>

YOU ARE **REWARDED EACH** AND **EVERY** TIME YOU...

DO THIS!

Mother Nature's
#1 Success Strategy
FIND YOUR REWARD INSIDE

10 TRAITS - LEADERS OF POWER AND COURAGE

RWANDA: A CASE HISTORY

A New Model of Prosperity and Leadership

Where in the world have women taken the lead? Rwanda.

In 2004, Rwanda's president Paul Kagame decided that the country had seen enough of war, bloodshed, and genocide. So a QUOTA requiring that 30% of members of Parliament be WOMEN was written into the Constitution.

Then he issued an invitation to the women of Rwanda to run for public office.

His invitation mobilized the women of Rwanda. In 2004, 30% of the elected members in Parliament were women. They became role-models of leadership for all women in the country.

In 2008, the number of women in Parliament jumped to 56%. When women in Parliament reached 56%, the focus of policies and monies shifted from weapons and warfare to education, healthcare, infrastructure and sustainability.

In this context, it is important to note that, in 2015, <u>America ranked #72</u> in the world, with only 19.4% women in Congress.

There are more than 50 Democracies around the world that have more women in leadership than the United States. We can do better. How much better? Let's aim for the TOP of the list. In 2015, Rwanda remains at the top, with 63.8% of its leaders, women.

ALEXIA PARKS

NOTES

10 TRAITS - LEADERS OF POWER AND COURAGE

RESOURCES

- 67% of college graduates are women (WomenMovingMillions.org)
- 72% of class valedictorians in 2011 were women (Women Will Rule the World; Newsweek)
- In the 21st Century, BRAINS count a lot more than brawn. "The Importance of Sex." (The Economist)
- Are Women Better Decision-Makers? (New York Times)
- Ann Cooper: Raised in a Matriarchal Society. Alexia Parks.
- The Key to Our Sustainability Lies Hardwired in the Female Brain. Alexia Parks
- The Chelsea Effect (The Guardian)
- Are American Women Ready for A Woman President? Economist YouGov Poll.
- In Brazil, the United Arab Emirates, and Russia, the vast majority of college graduates are female. (Newsweek)
- Today's economic growth is driven by women. (The Economist)
- "Studies show that women are more likely to spend money on improving health, education, infrastructure… and less likely to waste it on tanks and bombs." (The Economist)
- American women hold 89 percent of U.S. bank accounts and 51% of all personal wealth. (Influence, authors: Maddy Dychtwald, Christine Larson)
- "Women are the biggest emerging market in the history of the planet - more than twice the size of India and China combined. It's a seismic change, and by all indications, it will continue." (Influence)
- American women are responsible for 83% of all consumer purchases.
- Forget India, China, and the internet. The economic power of the world is now in the hands of women. (The Economist)
- A woman's natural leadership style is mentor-leadership. It is collaborative. In addition, women want to mentor and empower others. @alexiaparks
- "When the going gets tough, the FEMALE brain turns on!" @alexiaparks
- "Women are a national asset." Nancy Koehn quote, Harvard Business professor.

ALEXIA PARKS

- Women are hardwired by evolution with the traits of a great leader. (**Hardwired – The 10 Traits of Women**, author Alexia Parks)
- The primary love of women? Women are hardwired to affirm life. They have a natural love of people, diversity, and community. (Oxford University, University College of London, Hardwired – The 10 Traits)
- The primary love of men? Tools, technology, and inanimate objects. (Oxford University, Univ. College of London, Hardwired The 10 Traits)
- The Leadership GENE. Scientists Find DNA Sequence Associated With Leadership (Lead scientist Dr Jan-Emmanuel De Neve, from University College London, and Alexia Parks, Hardwired The 10 Traits)

10 TRAITS Leadership Institute Watch: Video (3-Min) Alexia Parks

BUSINESS:

- Faith Popcorn on the Corporate Man Cave. Faith Popcorn Brain Reserve
- 75% of the future workforce and consumers will not be white males. (James Turley, CEO Ernst & Young, Bloomberg)
- CEOs name top leadership traits that favor women. BBC – Capital
- Only 16% of board members of mid-to-large U.S. businesses are women. (Bloomberg News)
- The European Union plans 40% boardroom quotas for women. (New York Times)
- Companies with women as directors are more successful. (Bloomberg)
- Women need more business support. In the U.S. only 20% of firms with revenues over $1 million are women owned. (Council of PR Firms)
- Bianca Griffith - Social Impact Entrepreneurship - A Case History
- YouTube: You Have the Power to Control Your Destiny. Rehmah Kasule, Global Women's Leadership #1 Award Winner 2014 - Goldman Sachs & Fortune Magazine "Most Powerful Women in the World Summit." *Note: Alexia Parks is a United Nations - UN-Habitat Virtual Mentor To Rehmah Kasule 2014-2015.*

10 TRAITS - LEADERS OF POWER AND COURAGE

- Rehmah Kasule: CEDA-Uganda.org - A Case History
- Irene Vilar: America's Latino EcoFestival - A Case History
- Female-owned small businesses, now just 16% of total U.S. employment, will be responsible for creating one-third of the 15.3 million new jobs by 2018. (Forbes; US Labor Bureau)
- Of 8 million new jobs created in the EU since 2000, 75% went to women. (Newsweek)
- Women are becoming more educated and exhibiting leadership skills, yet few are elected or invited into key decision-making roles.
- "Women are slowly running out of patience everywhere." Viviane Reding EU Justice Commissioner.
- "There must be an increase in the number of leadership positions open to women." Catalyst.org calls for 25% women on FP500 boards by 2017.
- "There needs to be a measurement of goals and milestones met." (Catalyst)
- Your Amazing Career Starts Now - Review of Sheryl Sanberg book.
- Elevate Your Career, Levo League is a community dedicated to the career success of Gen Y women.
- Leadership from the Foot of the Table

POLITICS:

- Men Rule: A Report by The Women & Politics Institute, School of Public Affairs, at American University; & Loyola Marymount University. 2012) 67% of women need confidence boosting and leadership training. Women need to be "invited" or "asked" to lead.
- A historic win in 2012, yet only 17% of the members of the U.S. House of Representatives are women. 20% in the Senate.
- The U.S. ranks #72 in the world in terms of women leaders in government in 2015
- 50 Democracies. There are 50 democracies around the world that have a higher ranking than the U.S. (Women in Parliaments; Inter-Parliamentary Union)
- Why 56%? It is a tipping point.

- Rwanda ranks #1 in the world in 2015, with 63.8% women in parliament.

ALEXIA PARKS

- In the U.S., only <u>277 women have been elected to the U.S. Congress</u> vs 12,000 men, since 1920.

LINKS to Additional Articles & Books:

Hardwired – The 10 Major Traits of Women Hardwired by Evolution That Can Save the World – Author, Alexia Parks
19 Percent of Congress is Female. Why not half? – Kate Sheppard, Mother Jones
Influence – How Women's Soaring Economic Power Will Transform Our World for the Better – Maddy Dychtwald, and Christine Larson
The End of Men The Beginning of Women – Hanna Rosin, senior editor The Atlantic, co-founder of Slate's Double X
Lean In: Women, Work, and the Will to Lead – Sheryl Sandberg
<u>**Shared Traits that Unite Women in Power**</u> (Fast Company)

<u>**A Complete List of Alexia Parks Articles on the Huffington Post**</u>

WEB: <u>AlexiaParks.com</u>

10 TRAITS - LEADERS OF POWER AND COURAGE

Alexia Parks 10 TRAITS – Blog, Virtual Mentors, Virtual Mentor Office Hours and Leadership Training: AlexiaParks.com

BOOKS by Alexia Parks

HARDWIRED: The 10 Major Traits of Women Hardwired By Evolution That Can Transform the World

OM Money Money – Transforming the Way You Work (E-book)

Parkinomics: 8 GREAT Ways to Thrive in the New Economy (Amazon Bestseller)

Dr Joel's Be Super Fit™ for Life!

Focus on Success: A 10 Step Mentoring System for Schools

An American GULAG: Secret P.O.W. Camps for Teens

10 Golden Rules That Guide Loving Families (English/Spanish)

Rapid Evolution: Seven Words That Will Change Your Life Forever!

10 Golden Rules That Guide Teacher-Mentors (2015)

How Changing Your Name Can Change Your Life (2016)

People Heaters: How to Keep Warm in Winter

How Love Heals

Twitter: @alexiaparks

WEB: AlexiaParks.com

Made in the USA
San Bernardino, CA
24 December 2016